my big SCi

ence book

Simon Mugford

priddy books
big ideas for little people

Contents

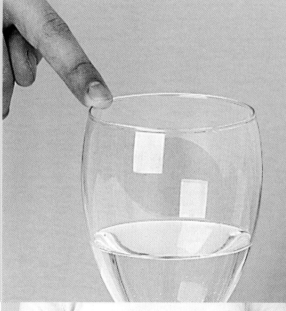

Note to parents

The experiments in this book will introduce children to simple scientific concepts and prompt them to explore and question the world around them. Many of the experiments will surprise children and adults alike, so get ready to have fun together.

Designed by Neville Graham and Emmett Kenny
Photography by Richard Brown

This book was made by Roger Priddy, Robert Tainsh, Jo Douglass and Louisa Beaumont.

We hope you enjoy this book as much as we enjoyed making it.

Agency photographs:
p.25 middle right, David Nunuk (Science Photo Library)
p.26 middle right, Damien Lovegrove (Science Photo Library)
p.37 middle right, Blair Seitz (Science Photo Library)
p.50 bottom left, John Daniels (Ardea, London)
Additional photography on pages 9, 19, 59, 65, 67, 70, 71 and 75 © Digital Vision

Copyright © 2003 St. Martin's Press
Published by

priddy books

4 Crinan Street, London, N1 9XW
A division of Macmillan Publishers Ltd

What you need

Starting your science lab

Getting started

All of the experiments in this book can be carried out with things you can find at home or in your local store. Many of the things you will need are shown on these pages, but check the 'You will need' section at the beginning of each experiment before you begin. Always ask before using anything at home!

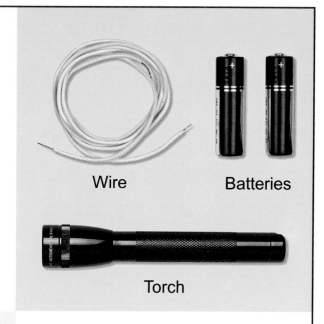

Wire

Batteries

Torch

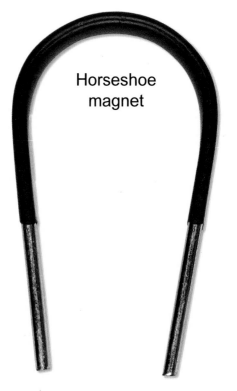

Horseshoe magnet

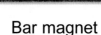

Bar magnet

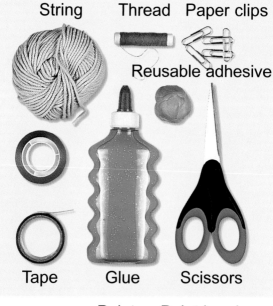

String

Thread

Paper clips

Reusable adhesive

Tape

Glue

Scissors

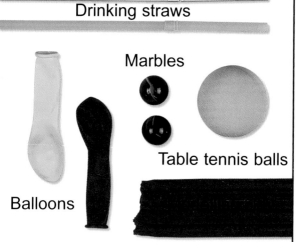

Drinking straws

Marbles

Table tennis balls

Balloons

Colouring pencils

Paints

Paint brushes

Colouring pens

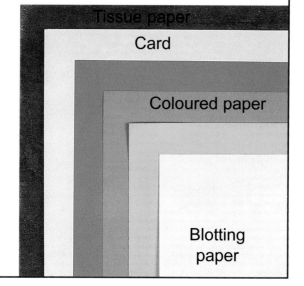

Tissue paper

Card

Coloured paper

Blotting paper

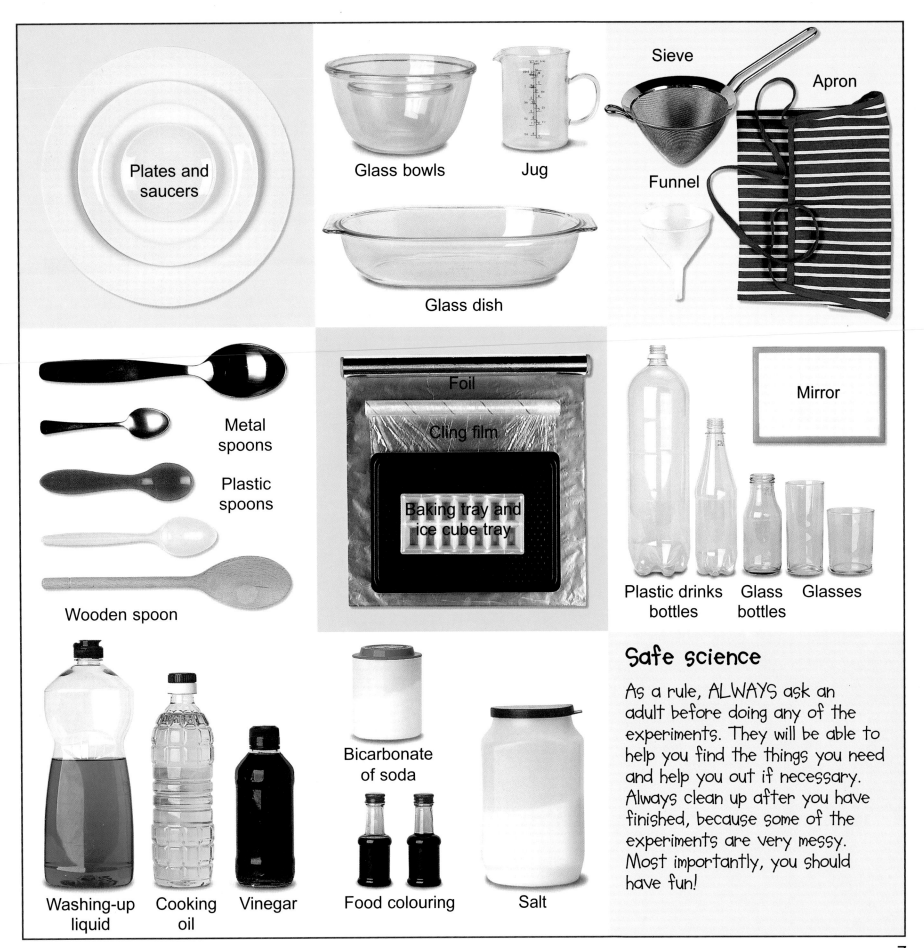

Plates and saucers

Glass bowls

Jug

Sieve

Funnel

Apron

Glass dish

Metal spoons

Plastic spoons

Wooden spoon

Foil

Cling film

Baking tray and ice cube tray

Mirror

Plastic drinks bottles

Glass bottles

Glasses

Washing-up liquid

Cooking oil

Vinegar

Bicarbonate of soda

Food colouring

Salt

Safe science

As a rule, ALWAYS ask an adult before doing any of the experiments. They will be able to help you find the things you need and help you out if necessary. Always clean up after you have finished, because some of the experiments are very messy. Most importantly, you should have fun!

Rocket **balloon**

Make a balloon that flies like a rocket

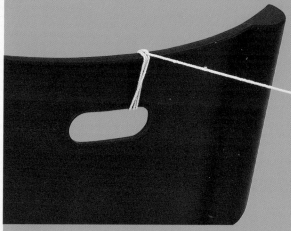

1 Tie one end of the string to the back of a chair.

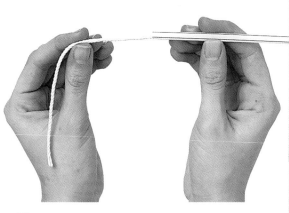

2 Thread the straw onto the string and tie the other end of the string to the other chair.

3 Attach two pieces of tape to the straw as shown.

4 Inflate the balloon, hold the opening, and attach it to the straw with the tape.

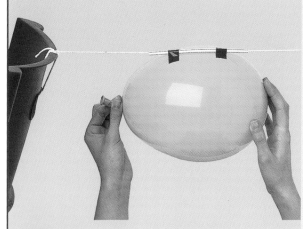

5 Pull the balloon to one end of the string and let go. What happens?

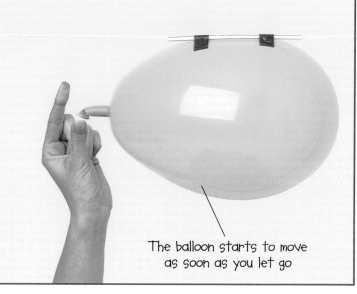

The balloon starts to move as soon as you let go

8

The balloon moves in the opposite direction to the airflow

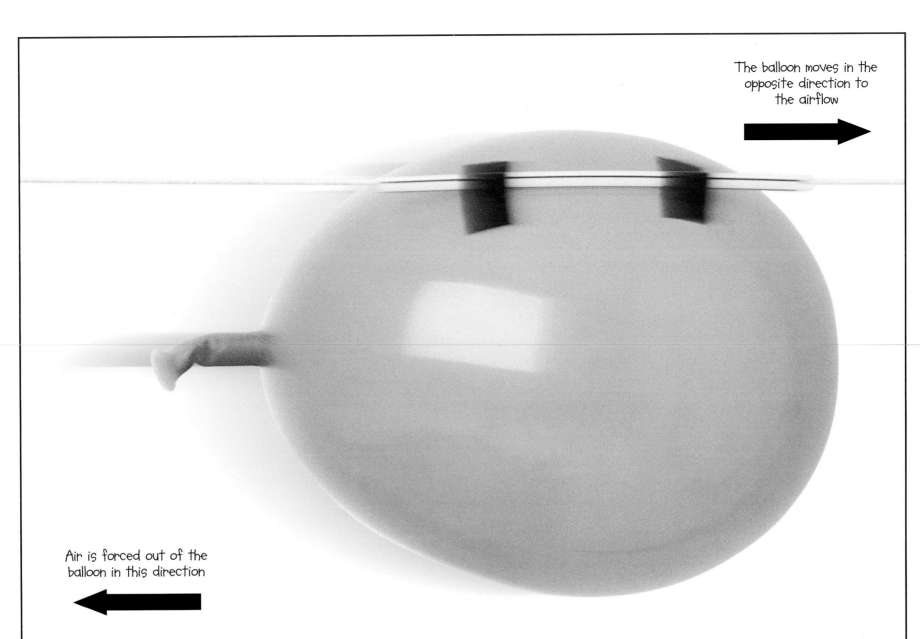

Air is forced out of the balloon in this direction

Action and reaction

To make something move one way, a force has to work in the opposite direction – this is known as 'action and reaction.' The air inside the inflated balloon is pushing in all directions. When you let go of the balloon, air rushes out the hole, creating a pushing force in the opposite direction. This makes the balloon move.

Rockets

Real rockets work in a similar way to your rocket balloon. A rocket engine works by exploding fuel inside a chamber that is open at the bottom. The force of the exploding fuel coming out of the rocket creates an opposite force that pushes the rocket up and on into space.

9

Bottle **diver**

Make your own deep sea diver

You will need:

- large plastic drinks bottle
- water
- thick foil (a disposable food tray is ideal)
- flexible drinking straw
- reusable adhesive
- glass
- paper clip
- scissors
- pen

1 Trace or copy this shape of the diver onto a piece of foil.

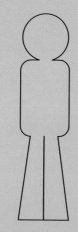

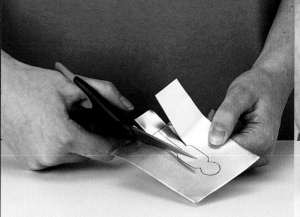

2 Carefully cut around the outline of the diver.

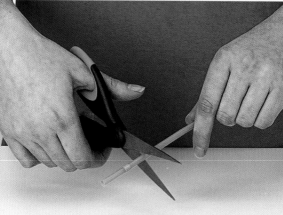

3 Cut out the flexible section of the straw, leaving about two cm of straw on either side.

4 Bend the straw, and push each end onto the paper clip.

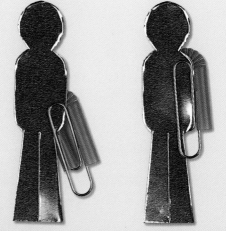

5 Carefully slide the straw onto the diver as shown.

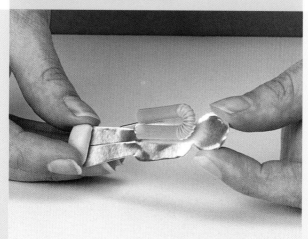

6 Stick a small piece of reusable adhesive onto the diver's feet.

7 Place the diver in a glass of water to make sure it floats.

8 Fill the bottle with water right to the top. Put the diver in and screw the lid on tightly.

9 Squeeze the bottle. What happens? Can you make the diver float anywhere in the bottle?

Density and diving

The air inside the bent straw is less dense (packed together) than the water around it. This makes the diver float. Squeezing the bottle forces water into the straw, making it more dense inside. This makes the diver sink. When you stop squeezing, the water density in the straw decreases and the diver floats to the top.

Floating fish

Fish make themselves float and sink by breathing gases in and out of an organ called a swim bladder. Breathing in gas makes the fish less dense, so it floats. Breathing the gas out makes it sink.

Sky diver

Make a model parachute

You will need:

- piece of polythene about 40 cm square (a plastic bag is ideal)
- 4 x 30 cm pieces of thread
- modelling clay
- scissors
- paper clip

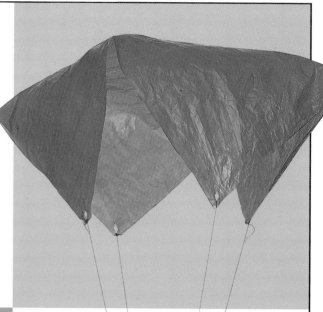

1 Cut a hole in each corner of the polythene. Attach a piece of thread to each corner.

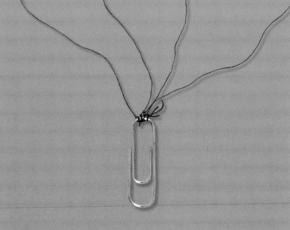

2 Tie each piece of thread to the paper clip. This is the 'harness' for your sky diver.

3 Make your sky diver out of a piece of modelling clay.

4 Press the paper clip into your sky diver. Fold the parachute and throw it as high as you can.

Air and drag

The parachute and sky diver are pulled to the ground by the force of gravity. As they fall, the air trapped beneath the parachute pushes up slightly, slowing down the parachute's fall. The force of the air pushing against the parachute is called air resistance, or drag.

Floating **test**

Why do some things float?

Float or sink?

Whether things float or sink depends upon their density – how tightly packed together the material inside it is. Metal ships are very heavy, but they are big and hollow (not very dense). This is how they are able to float on the sea.

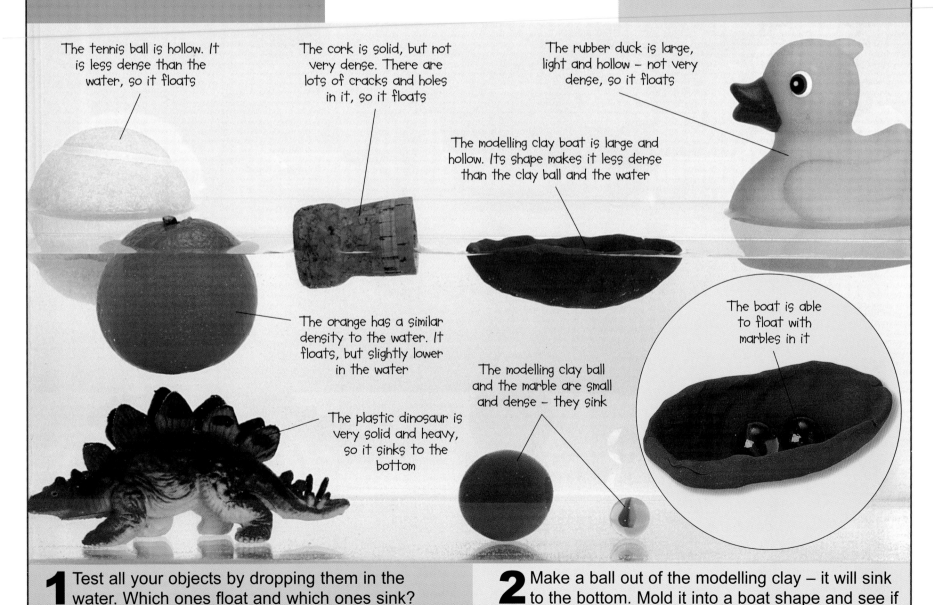

The tennis ball is hollow. It is less dense than the water, so it floats

The cork is solid, but not very dense. There are lots of cracks and holes in it, so it floats

The rubber duck is large, light and hollow – not very dense, so it floats

The modelling clay boat is large and hollow. Its shape makes it less dense than the clay ball and the water

The orange has a similar density to the water. It floats, but slightly lower in the water

The modelling clay ball and the marble are small and dense – they sink

The plastic dinosaur is very solid and heavy, so it sinks to the bottom

The boat is able to float with marbles in it

1 Test all your objects by dropping them in the water. Which ones float and which ones sink?

2 Make a ball out of the modelling clay – it will sink to the bottom. Mold it into a boat shape and see if you can make it float with something in it.

Paper glider

Make a plane that really flies

You will need:

- piece of A4 paper
- paper clip

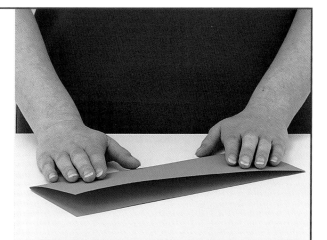

1 Fold the paper in half lengthways. Make sure the fold is as straight as possible. Then unfold the paper.

2 Fold one corner in so that its edge meets the fold. Do the same with the opposite corner.

3 Fold the paper back along the first fold that you made.

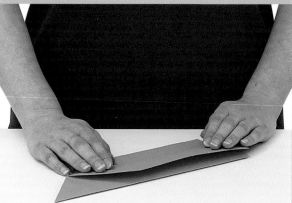

4 Fold one side down to meet the first fold. Turn it over and do the same on the other side.

5 Push a paper clip onto the nose of your plane. Now your plane is ready to fly.

Aerodynamics

The paper glider flies through the air because of its pointed shape. This is called an aerodynamic design. As it cuts through the air, the air beneath its wings pushes the glider up – in the opposite direction to the force of gravity, which is pulling it to the ground.

Gyro-copter

Make a spinning, flying machine

You will need:

- piece of paper (about 20 cm x 15 cm)
- pen or pencil
- scissors
- paper clip

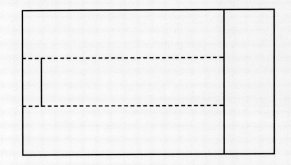

1 Carefully copy this pattern onto your piece of paper.

2 Cut along the two dotted lines as shown above.

3 Fold one of the flaps along the solid black line.

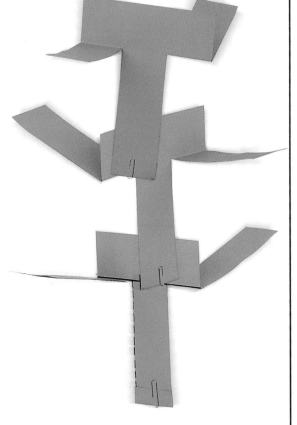

4 Turn the gyrocopter over and fold over the second flap.

5 Fold over the small flap at the bottom, and slide on the paper clip. Throw it into the air as high as you can.

Spinning wings

As your gyrocopter falls, air pushing against the wings makes them spin. The spinning wings have the effect of slowing its fall to the ground.

Air action

How does air make things fly?

You will need:

- 2 table tennis balls
- balloon
- hairdryer
- thread
- drinking straw
- scissors
- tape

Pressure points

The faster that air is moving, the lower its pressure. High-pressure air moves towards low-pressure air, and anything in between will be pushed as well. Blowing between the table tennis balls reduces the air pressure between them, so the high-pressure air on either side pushes them together.

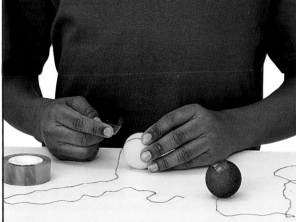

1 Cut two pieces of thread, each about 20 cm long. Tape them to the table tennis balls.

2 Tie the threads to something, about 10 cm apart. Allow the balls to hang at the same height.

3 Hold the drinking straw about 10 cm behind the balls and blow between them.

4 The balls should move together. Why do you think that happens?

The table tennis ball 'floats' in the airflow

The balloon floats higher than the table tennis ball

The airflow keeps the balloon afloat, even at an angle

5 Point the hairdryer upwards, switch it on and put a table tennis ball in the airflow.

6 Now do the same with a balloon. What happens?

7 Try tilting the hairdryer to one side. Can you keep the balloon in the airflow?

Air moves quicker over the top of a wing than it does below

Aerofoil

Slower moving air below the wing means the pressure here is higher than it is above

High pressure pushes the wing, and the airplane up

Floating and flying

The air moving upwards hits the bottom of the ball or balloon and slows down, which creates an area of higher pressure. The high-pressure air pushes up against gravity, which is pulling the ball or balloon down. This effect is used in aeroplane wings to make them fly. The curved shape of a wing is called an aerofoil.

17

Bridge shapes

Find out how bridges stay up

You will need:

- 6 pieces of A4 card
- 8 books of the same size
- tape
- objects to test the strength of the bridges

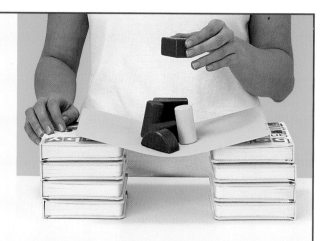

1 Place a piece of card across two piles of books. How much weight will the bridge hold?

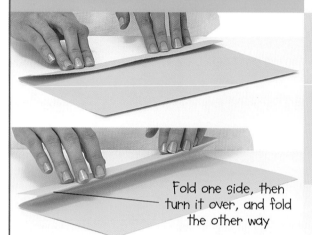

Fold one side, then turn it over, and fold the other way

2 Fold a second piece of card lengthways into a zig-zag shape as shown.

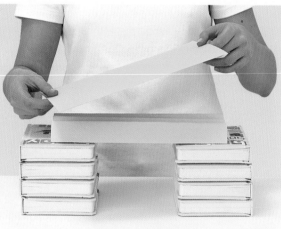

3 Place the zig-zag shape across the books. Then place another piece of card on top.

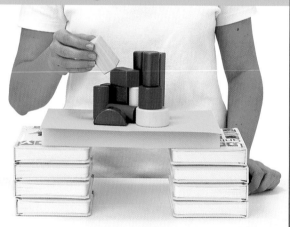

4 Put some weights on top of the bridge. Does it hold more or less weight than the first bridge?

Bend the top piece of card and tape it down to make an arch

5 Place one piece of card on top of the other, about three cm from the end. Tape it down.

Complete your arch bridge by placing another piece of card on top

6 Place the ends of the arch on top of half of the books. Put the remaining books on top to hold it.

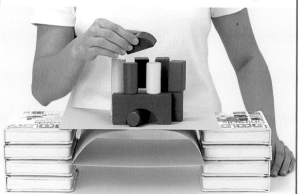

7 Put some weights on top of your arch bridge. How much weight does it hold?

The bridge is only supported at the sides, so the weight pushes it down in the middle

Balanced forces

Bridges support their own weight as well as the things that go across them. They do this by spreading the force of the weight through the bridge. The bridge structure 'pushes' against the force and the weight is supported. These are called balanced forces.

Strong triangles

The triangular shapes in this suspension bridge are keeping the forces balanced.

The triangular shapes in the zig-zag section spread the force of the weight across the bridge

Arch bridges

Arch shapes are often used to provide strength in bridges and other structures.

The arch shape spreads the force of the weight to the books

Balancing **act**

Make an acrobatic clown

You will need:

- paper
- colouring pens
- 2 small coins
- glue
- scissors

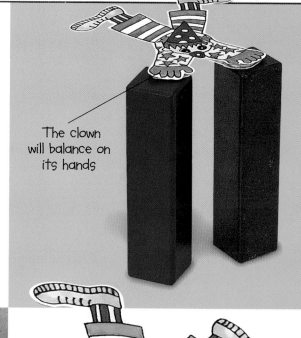

The clown will balance on its hands

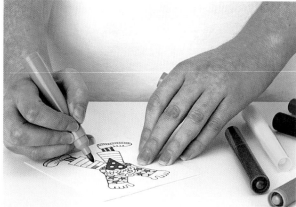

1 Make two copies of this picture on a piece of white paper.

2 Cut out both of the clown shapes and colour them in.

Balance the clown on its nose on the end of a straw, pencil, or finger

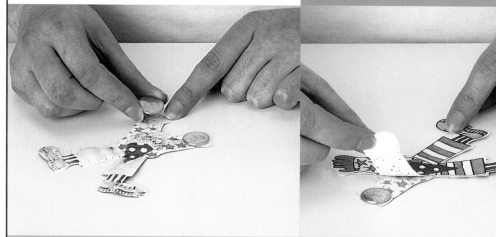

3 Place one shape face down on a table. Cover it with glue and place the coins on the clown's hands.

4 Place the other shape on top (coloured side up). Line up the edges and leave it to dry.

Balancing act

The coins placed between the clown's hands have shifted the centre of gravity – the point where the weight is focused. As long as the centre of gravity is over an object, the clown will remain balanced and will not fall off.

Seeing sound

How does sound make movement?

You will need:

- bowl
- cling film
- rice
- metal tray
- metal spoon

Visual vibrations

Hitting the tray with the spoon makes the air around it vibrate (move around very quickly). The air travels in waves in all directions. When the sound waves reach the cling film, they make it vibrate, which makes the rice move. Our ears pick up sounds in this way.

1 Stretch a piece of cling film over the bowl as tightly as you can.

2 Scatter some grains of rice across the top of the cling film.

3 Hold the metal tray close to the bowl. Strike the tray with the spoon to make a loud noise. What happens to the rice?

Phone a friend

Make a string telephone

You will need:

- 2 strong paper cups
- piece of string (at least 3 metres long)
- scissors
- sharp pencil
- a friend

String vibrations

Sound waves travel through solid objects better than they do through the air. Speaking into a cup makes it vibrate, which makes the string vibrate in turn. The vibrations travel along the string to the other cup, which vibrates and reproduces the sound.

1 Use a sharp pencil to make holes in the bottom of the cups. Push the string through each hole.

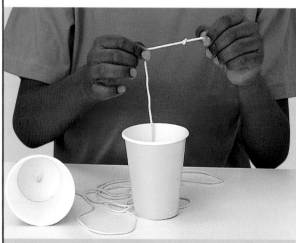

2 Tie a knot in each end of the string inside the cups. The knots must be bigger than the holes.

Speaking makes the string vibrate

Vibrations are turned back into sound by the cup

Vibrations travel along the string

3 Ask a friend to take one cup and move far enough away to make the string tight. One of you should speak into a cup, while the other holds their cup to their ear. Take turns speaking to one another.

Singing glass

Make a noise with a glass

You will need:

- glass with a long stem
- water

Good vibrations

The glass 'sings' because it is being made to vibrate by your moving finger. The sound you hear depends on the size and shape of the glass, and how much water is in it. A big glass filled with water will make a low note. A small glass with a little water will make a high note.

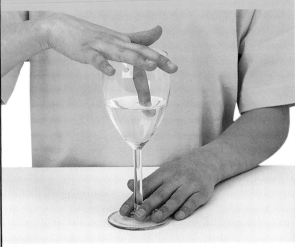

1 Half fill the glass with water. Dip your forefinger in it.

2 Hold the base of the glass firmly with one hand. Press down on the rim of the glass with your wet finger.

3 Slowly and steadily move your finger around the rim of the glass. It may take some practice, but you should be able to make a ringing sound come from the glass.

Bottle xylophone

Make music with bottles

You will need:

- 6 glass bottles
- wooden spoon
- water
- food colouring
- jug

Water music

Hitting the bottles with the spoon makes them vibrate and produce a sound. The more the bottle vibrates, the higher the note will be. The more water there is in a bottle, the less it vibrates, so less water means higher notes.

1 Fill one bottle with water. Fill each other bottle with slightly less than the bottle next to it.

2 Adding some food colouring will help you to see the different levels of water.

The less water there is in a bottle, the higher the note it will make

Tap each bottle with the spoon

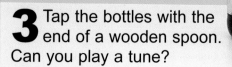

3 Tap the bottles with the end of a wooden spoon. Can you play a tune?

Looking at **light**

How does light behave?

You will need:

- torch
- mirror
- sheet of white paper

1 In a dark room, shine your torch at the wall. What happens if you move your torch?

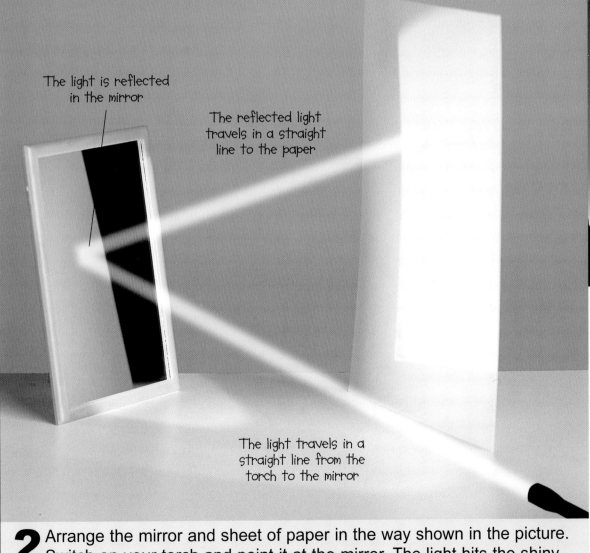

The light is reflected in the mirror

The reflected light travels in a straight line to the paper

The light travels in a straight line from the torch to the mirror

2 Arrange the mirror and sheet of paper in the way shown in the picture. Switch on your torch and point it at the mirror. The light hits the shiny surface of the mirror and is reflected at an angle to the paper.

Light lines

Light travels in a straight line until it hits an object. It also travels faster than anything else – about 186,000 miles a second. The stars that you see at night are so far away, that the light has taken many years to reach Earth, where we can see them.

Bending **light**

See how light can bend

You will need:

- glass
- water
- coloured pen

Refraction

The pen looks bent at the point where it enters the water. This is because the light is being slowed down as it passes through the water. The image of the pen at that point takes longer to reach our eyes. This effect is called refraction.

The pen looks straight

1 Put the pen in the glass as shown. It should look as normal.

The pen looks like it has a bend in it

2 Now fill the glass with water, almost to the top. Does the pen look any different?

Mirages

Refraction happens in air when there is a difference in temperature. In deserts, light travels quicker through the hot air near the ground than it does through the cooler air above it. This makes things look closer than they actually are, or it can look like there is a lake up ahead. This illusion is called a mirage.

Mirror writing

Trick your eyes and brain

You will need:

- mirror with stand
- books
- paper
- pen or pencil
- large piece of card

1 Make two piles of books of the same height. Put the piece of paper between the books.

2 Prop up the mirror behind the paper as shown.

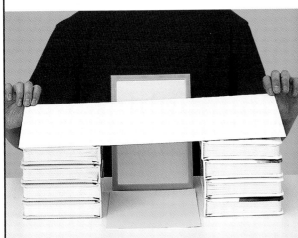

3 Put the large piece of card across the top of the books as shown above.

Reverse writing

Our eyes and brain are used to seeing the words written normally, so seeing them written backwards makes it difficult to recognise and write even simple things, such as your name.

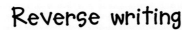

The mirror reflects your writing in the opposite direction, so everything appears backwards

4 Position yourself so that you can only see the paper in the mirror. Try writing your name while looking in the mirror. How easy is it to write?

Shadow **puppets**

Play with light to make shadows

You will need:

- card
- scissors
- drinking straws
- tape
- torch
- pen or pencil

1 Draw some shapes onto the card, or you could copy the shapes on these pages.

2 Carefully cut out the shapes.

The shapes cast shadows on the wall

3 Use tape to attach a drinking straw to one side of each of the shapes.

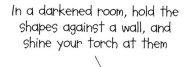

In a darkened room, hold the shapes against a wall, and shine your torch at them

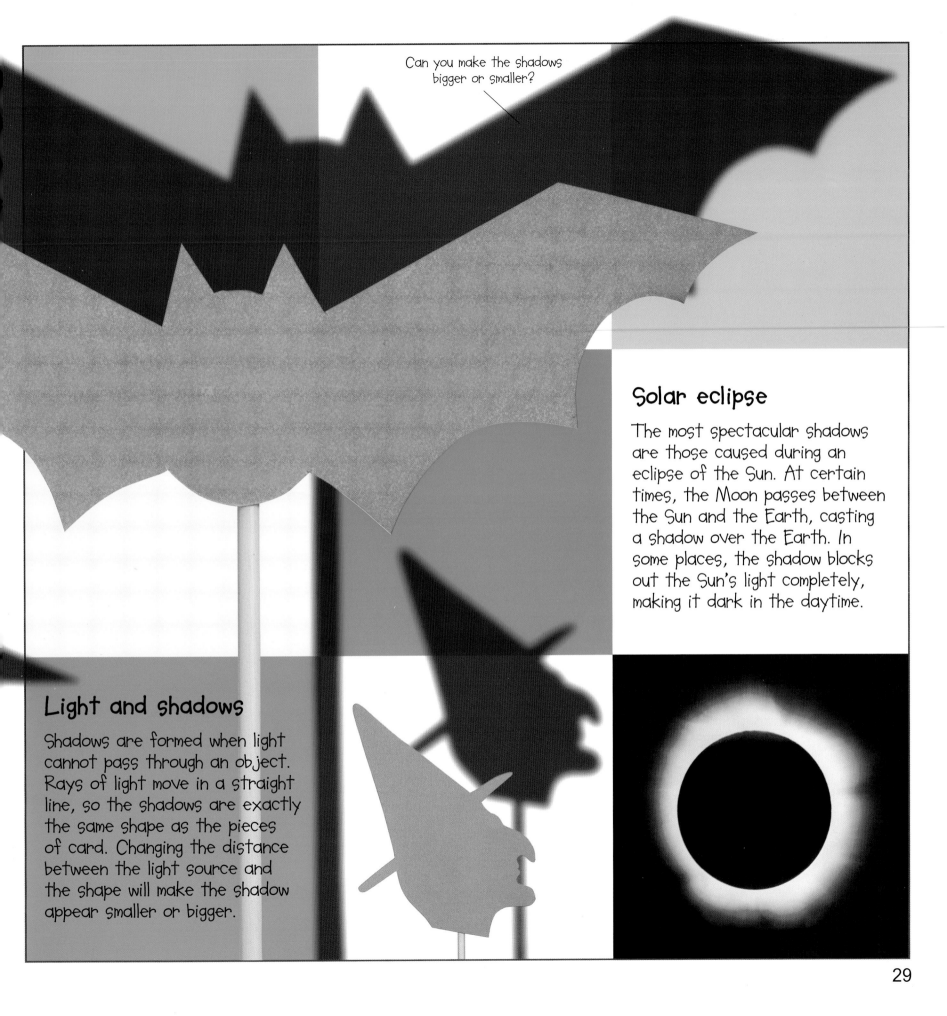

Can you make the shadows bigger or smaller?

Solar eclipse

The most spectacular shadows are those caused during an eclipse of the Sun. At certain times, the Moon passes between the Sun and the Earth, casting a shadow over the Earth. In some places, the shadow blocks out the Sun's light completely, making it dark in the daytime.

Light and shadows

Shadows are formed when light cannot pass through an object. Rays of light move in a straight line, so the shadows are exactly the same shape as the pieces of card. Changing the distance between the light source and the shape will make the shadow appear smaller or bigger.

29

Optical illusions

Play tricks with your eyes

Seeing sense

You will not believe your eyes when you look at the pictures and patterns on these pages. These optical illusions work by arranging shapes in ways that fool your eyes and brain. You might see things that are not there, twisted shapes and even moving objects. Have fun, but staring at them for too long could make your eyes hurt!

1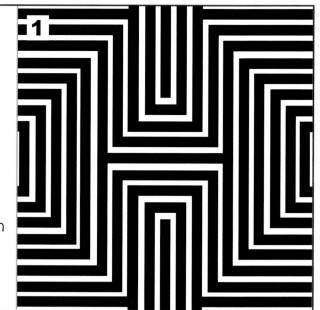

2

3

Seeing the invisible

1 Can you see the two diamond shapes? Can you see an outline?

2 You can see a triangle, but where is its outline?

3 Look at the points where the lines meet. Do you see circles?

4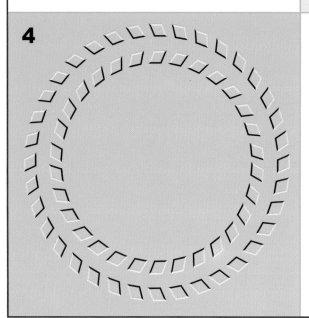

5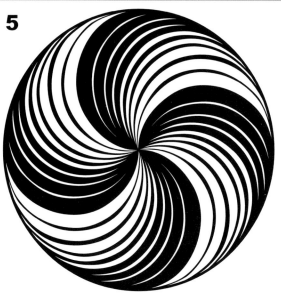

Moving circles

4 Stare at the centre of the circles, and move your head backwards and forwards. Do the circles appear to move?

5 Stare at the centre of the spiral spokes. Hold the page upright, and slowly twist it up and down. Do the spokes appear to twist and move?

6

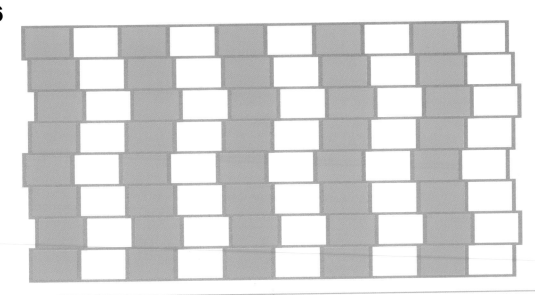

9

Straight lines?

6 The grey horizontal lines look like they slope. They are, in fact, absolutely straight.

7 The circles make the edges of the square appear to bend. They are perfectly straight.

7

10

Flashing spots

8 Can you see grey spots flashing in the white circles? Can you touch one? Probably not – once you try to focus on one grey spot, it disappears.

8

Two-in-one

9 What do you see? A rabbit or a duck?

10 Do you see a woman's face, or a man playing a saxophone?

More optical illusions
How are your eyes?

Spiral circles

1 At first glance, this illusion looks like a spiral. Take a closer look, and you will see that it is actually a series of circles. Follow them with your finger to check.

Big or small?

2 Which of the two black circles is the biggest? They are actually the same size.

3 How about the two green lines? Is one bigger than the other? Measure them with ruler to find out.

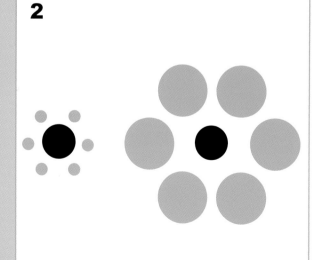

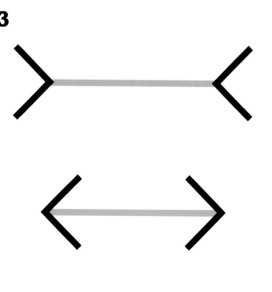

Picture mixer

Turn two pictures into one

You will need:

- paper
- pencil
- colouring pens
- scissors
- glue

The bird appears to be in the cage

1 Copy each one of these pictures onto two separate pieces of paper. Colour in the bird.

2 Cut each picture into a circle about eight cm across.

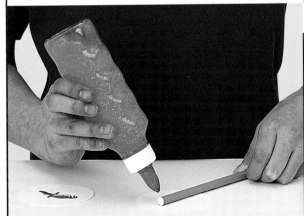

3 Lay one picture face down and cover it with glue. Put the pencil on it and stick on the other picture.

4 When the glue has dried, hold the pencil as shown. Rub your hands to make the picture spin.

Vision mix

We see the bird appear in the cage because the pictures are moving too quickly for our eyes and brain to tell the difference between the two. Cartoons and movies use this effect by moving a series of still pictures very quickly. This creates an illusion of movement.

Mixing colours

Mix paints to make new colours

You will need:

- paints: red, yellow, blue, white and black
  - brushes
  - paper

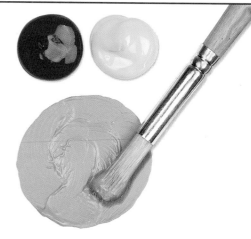

1 Mix together red and yellow. Which colour does it make?

2 How about mixing yellow and blue? What do you get?

3 Now try blue and red. Which colour do they make?

4 Now try three colours – red, yellow and blue. What does this make?

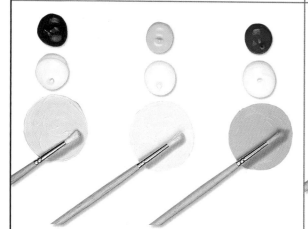

5 Try mixing some colours with white. Does it make the colours lighter or darker?

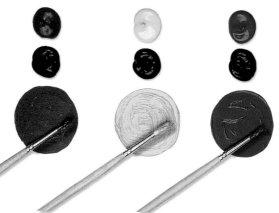

6 Now try mixing the same colours with black. What happens now?

Paints and pigments

The colours in paints and inks are produced by substances called pigments. Pigments absorb some colours and reflect their own. For example, red absorbs green and blue colour and reflects red. Mixtures of different pigments create new colours by absorbing and reflecting different mixtures of colour.

Colour wheel

See spinning colours mix

You will need:

- white card
- piece of string (about 1 to 2 metres long)
- sharp pencil
- scissors
- colouring pens
- a friend

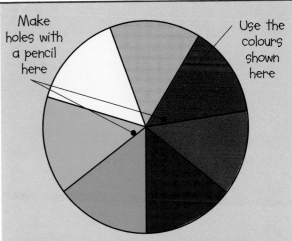

Make holes with a pencil here

Use the colours shown here

1 Copy this coloured disc onto a piece of card. Make it about eight cm across.

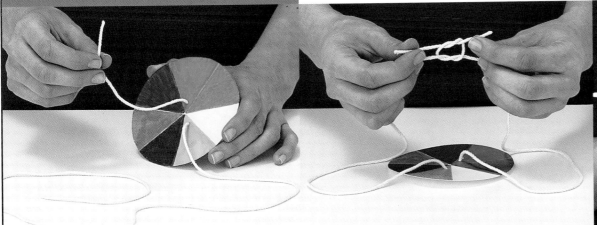

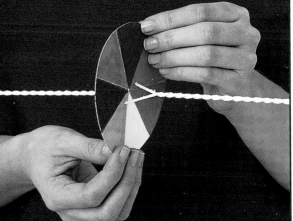

2 Push the string through one hole and then back through the other.

3 Tie the two ends together and position the wheel halfway along the string.

4 Take hold of the string loop and pull it tight. Ask your friend to twist the wheel.

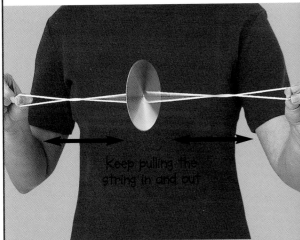

Keep pulling the string in and out

5 When your friend lets go of the wheel, pull the string in and out to keep the wheel turning.

As the wheel spins, the colours seem to merge together

White colours

White light is made up of several different colours, a bit like the colours on your wheel. When you make the colours spin, they move too quickly for our eyes and brain to pick them out separately, so we see them as a blurred, greyish white colour.

Pen colours

Discover the colours in pens

1 Cut out a piece of blotting paper. It should be big enough to fit around the inside of the glass.

Use five different colours

2 Draw five one-cm circles of colour, about four cm from the bottom of the paper.

3 Pour water into the glass, until it is about one to two cm deep. Stir in a teaspoon of salt.

4 Roll the paper into a tube and put it in the glass. Leave it for about 30 minutes. What happens?

Sweet colours

See the colours in sweets

Move the sweets around so that the colour runs into the water

1 Pour a few drops of water into a saucer, and add four or five sweets of the same colour.

Colours before being soaked in water

Chromatography

The colours used in pens and sweets are made up of several different substances called pigments. Different pigments move through the paper at different speeds, which shows the various shades that make up the colours. This is called chromatography. Scientists called chemists often use chromatography to identify different chemicals in substances.

Green splits into blue and yellow pigments

Dark colours such as black and brown contain the most pigments

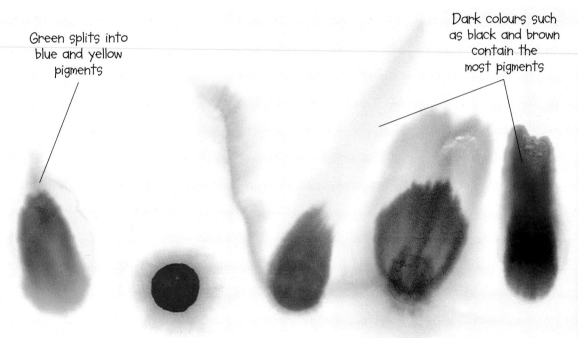

The colours split as they are drawn up through the paper

The brown colour contains blue pigment

2 Cut a strip of blotting paper and place one end in the coloured water. Leave it to stand.

Orange contains some red pigment

Try some other colours – orange...

Some colours contain only one pigment

...or perhaps blue.

Changing **states**

Three experiments about solids, liquids and gases

You will need:

- water
- ice cube tray
- freezer
- food colouring
- jug
- plate
- saucepan lid
- boiling water
- plastic drinks bottle

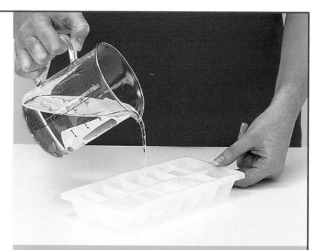

1 Fill an ice cube tray with water. Do not fill it to the top.

2 Add different colours of food colouring to the water. Leave the tray in the freezer overnight.

3 Take the tray out of the freezer. The water will have frozen into ice. Put the ice cubes on a plate.

4 As the ice warms up, it melts and changes back into water.

1 Ask an adult to fill a jug with boiling water. Hold a saucepan lid over it for about 20 seconds.

2 Take the lid away and look underneath. The steam has cooled and turned back into water.

Hot and cold

Water can be a solid, a liquid or a gas. A change in temperature can change it from one state to another. When it gets very cold, water freezes into solid ice, which melts back into a liquid when it gets warmer. Boiling water turns into a gas (steam) – this is called evaporation. As it cools, it returns to a liquid state. This process is called condensation.

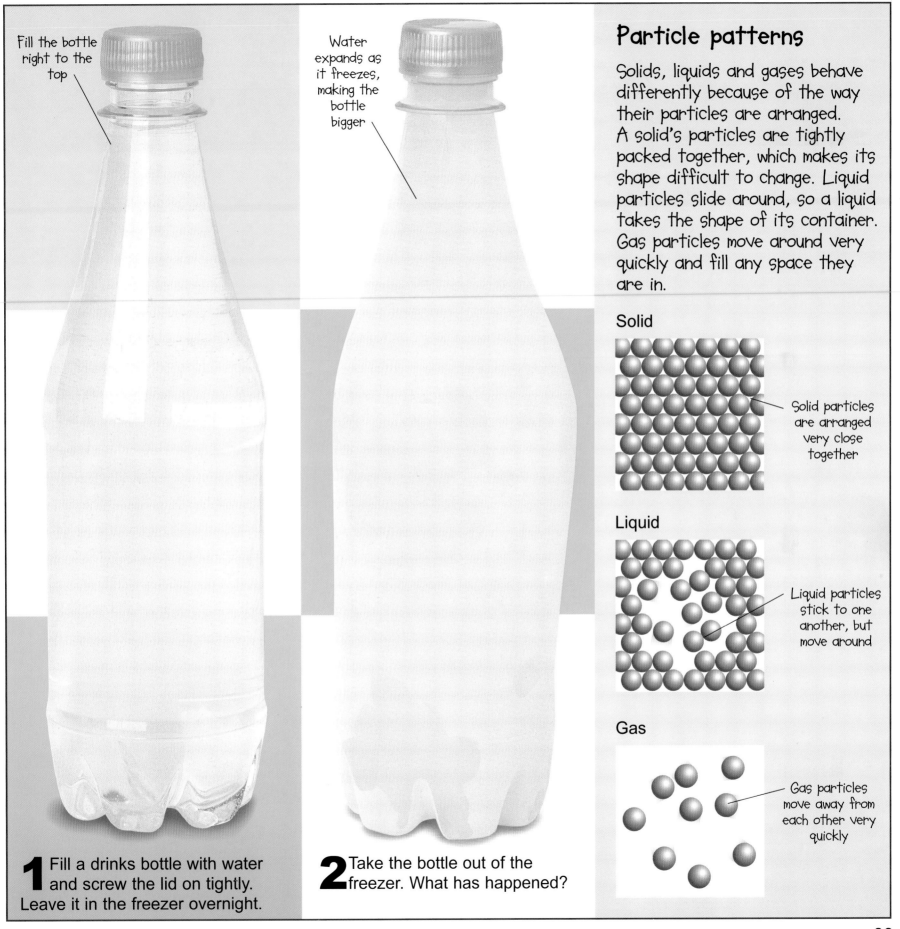

Fill the bottle right to the top

Water expands as it freezes, making the bottle bigger

Particle patterns

Solids, liquids and gases behave differently because of the way their particles are arranged. A solid's particles are tightly packed together, which makes its shape difficult to change. Liquid particles slide around, so a liquid takes the shape of its container. Gas particles move around very quickly and fill any space they are in.

Solid

Solid particles are arranged very close together

Liquid

Liquid particles stick to one another, but move around

Gas

Gas particles move away from each other very quickly

1 Fill a drinks bottle with water and screw the lid on tightly. Leave it in the freezer overnight.

2 Take the bottle out of the freezer. What has happened?

39

Liquid mix

Do all liquids mix together?

You will need:

- glasses
- teaspoon
- water
- apple juice
- cooking oil
- washing-up liquid

Liquid mixtures

Apple juice and water are very similar liquids and mix together easily. Oil does not dissolve in water, but adding some washing-up liquid makes the droplets of oil mix into the water – at least for a while. This type of mixture is called an emulsion.

Apple juice

Cooking oil

Washing-up liquid

1 Pour some water into a glass. Add some apple juice and stir.

2 Pour water into a second glass. Next, pour in some cooking oil.

3 Add some washing-up liquid to the water and oil. Give it a stir.

Apple juice mixes easily with water – these are called miscible liquids

Water and oil do not mix together – they are called immiscible liquids

Washing-up liquid is an emulsifier – it makes the oil and water mix

Solid test

Which solids dissolve in water?

You will need:

- glasses
- hot and cold water
- teaspoon
- substances to dissolve – salt, sugar, sand, instant coffee, custard powder, soap powder

Dissolving solids

Try mixing various substances in glasses of hot and cold water. Salt, sugar, coffee and soap powder are soluble – they will dissolve easily in water, especially if it is hot. Custard powder contains dried egg, which starts to cook in hot water. Sand is insoluble – it will not dissolve in water, whether it is hot or cold.

Instant coffee
Cold   Hot

Sugar
Cold   Hot

Custard powder
Cold   Hot

Salt
Cold   Hot

Sand
Cold   Hot

Soap powder
Cold   Hot

Oil bubbles

An oil and water spectacular!

You will need:

- large jar
- water
- cooking oil
- salt
- tablespoon
- jug

Dissolving and mixing

The liquids and dissolving experiments showed that oil and water will not mix together and that salt dissolves in water. In this experiment, the salt sinks to the bottom of jar, taking small amounts of oil with it. As the salt dissolves, the oil rises back to the surface, creating the strange bubbling effect.

1 Fill the jar three-quarters full of water. Add enough cooking oil to make a five-cm layer on top.

2 Next, add three to four tablespoons of salt and watch what happens.

The salt takes the oil down through the water

The oil floats back to the surface when the salt dissolves

Moving **heat**

What gets hot the quickest?

You will need:

- bowl
- boiling water
- wooden spoon
- metal spoon
- plastic spoon
- dried peas
- butter

Conduction

The way that heat moves through solid objects is called conduction. Some materials are better conductors than others. Metal is a very good conductor – this is why the butter on the metal spoon melts first. Wood and plastic are poor heat conductors, so it takes longer for the butter to melt on them.

1 Use a small piece of butter to stick a dried pea to each of the spoons.

2 Ask an adult to fill the bowl with boiling water. Then put the spoons in the bowl.

The metal spoon conducts the heat best

3 Leave the spoons for a while. Which pea starts to move first?

43

Balloon blow-up

Inflate a balloon without touching it

You will need:

- small drinks bottle
- balloon
- bicarbonate of soda
- vinegar
- funnel
- teaspoon

1 Using a funnel, pour about a third of a cup of vinegar into the bottle.

2 Slide the balloon onto the funnel as shown here.

3 Put two teaspoons of bicarbonate of soda into the balloon. Remove the funnel from the balloon.

4 Stretch the mouth of the balloon over the bottle, taking care not to let any of the bicarbonate of soda drop into it. You might need an adult to help you with this.

5 Hold the bottle, lift up the balloon and empty the bicarbonate of soda into the vinegar.

6 The bicarbonate of soda and vinegar will foam in the bottle. What happens to the balloon?

Gas balloon

When the bicarbonate of soda and vinegar mix together, they create a gas called carbon dioxide. All gases expand to fill any space available, so the carbon dioxide inflates the balloon.

The carbon dioxide gas produced by the bicarbonate of soda and vinegar inflates the balloon

Vinegar volcano

Make a volcano erupt in your kitchen

You will need:

- two small plastic drinks bottles
- large piece of card
- vinegar
- bicarbonate of soda
- tablespoon
- teaspoon
- food colouring
- washing-up liquid
- large plate or tray
- funnel
- pen or pencil
- scissors
- tape

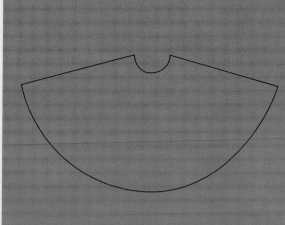

1 Copy this shape onto the card. It needs to be big enough to fit around the bottle.

2 Cut out the shape and bend it into a cone as shown. Secure it with tape.

3 Using a funnel, fill one of the bottles until it is about one-third full of vinegar.

4 Add a few drops of food colouring. We used red, but you can use any colour.

5 Add one tablespoon of washing-up liquid, and put the bottle to one side.

6 Put the second bottle on a tray and pour in three teaspoons of bicarbonate of soda.

7 Place the card cone over the bottle. Make sure the hole is level with the bottle opening.

8 Using a funnel, pour in the vinegar and washing-up liquid mixture. Remove the funnel and wait!

Warning!

This experiment will make a mess — remember to clean up afterwards!

The mixture comes out of the bottle

Gases and bubbles

When the vinegar and biacarbonate of soda mix together, they produce carbon dioxide gas. This gas creates bubbles in the vinegar and the washing-up liquid. The foaming, messy mixture expands and forces itself out of the top of the bottle.

The mixture oozes down the cone

Carbon dioxide gas forms bubbles in the mixture

47

Acid test

Are things acids or alkalis?

You will need:

- red cabbage
- 2 jugs
- sieve
- 5 glasses
- hot water
- test substances: vinegar, lemon juice, antacid liquid, bicarbonate of soda

Cabbage juice indicator

1 Tear up the red cabbage into small pieces, and put them in one of the jugs.

2 Pour in enough hot water to cover the cabbage. Let it stand for about 30 minutes.

Antacid liquid turns it light blue

3 Strain the cabbage juice into the other jug.

4 Pour the cabbage juice into five glasses.

Antacid liquid

5 Add one test substance to each of the glasses. Compare the results with the cabbage juice.

Acids and alkalis

Acids and alkalis are strong chemicals, but weak forms are found in all sorts of substances. Acids, such as lemon juice and vinegar, turn the cabbage juice a red colour. The antacid liquid and bicarbonate of soda are alkalis, and turn the juice blue. Acids and alkalis cancel each other out when mixed together.

Stinging things

The stings of bees and wasps are both very painful, but for different reasons. Bee stings contain acid, and an alkali such as soap will help ease the pain. Wasp stings contain strong alkalis, so an acid such as vinegar will help to stop the stinging.

Bee

Wasp

Bicarbonate of soda turns it blue

Vinegar turns it dark red

Lemon juice turns it light red

Bicarbonate of soda

Vinegar

Lemon juice

Magic **milk**

Make a colourful milk mixture

You will need:

- plate
- milk
- food colouring
- washing-up liquid

1 Pour some milk onto the plate. Make sure it fills to the rim.

2 Add some drops of food colouring to the milk. Use a few different colours if you can.

3 Drop a small amount of washing-up liquid onto the centre of the mixture.

The washing-up liquid breaks the surface tension

Pond skaters

The surface tension of water is strong enough to support small insects, such as this pond skater.

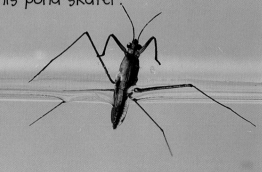

Surface tension

The molecules (the smallest parts) of the milk pull each other together, which stretches the surface of the milk into an invisible skin. This effect is called surface tension. Adding the washing-up liquid weakens the surface tension and makes the molecules move around. This makes the food colouring mix together.

The milk molecules move apart

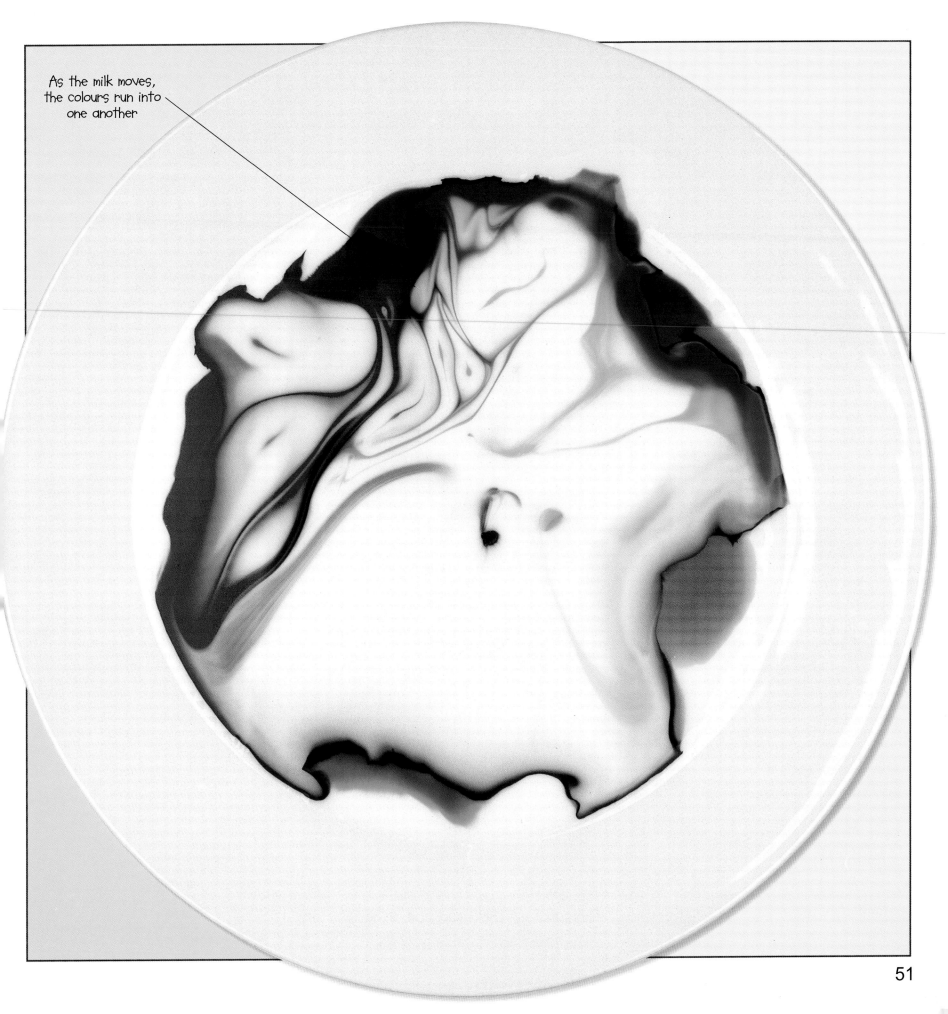

As the milk moves, the colours run into one another

Giant bubbles

Make huge water bubbles

You will need:

- washing-up liquid
- water
- glycerine or corn syrup
- large bowl (or a large pizza tray, if you want to make less mixture)
- wire coat hanger
- ball of string
- electrical tape
- jug

About bubble mixture

To make really good bubbles, for every 15 parts of water, mix in one part of washing-up liquid and a quarter part of glycerine. You can buy glycerine from chemists, but it is quite expensive, so if you plan to make lots of bubbles, corn syrup is a good, cheaper substitute.

Bubble mixture can be kept for several days. Give it a stir before each use

1 Mix the washing-up liquid and the glycerine in a jug. Stir it into a bowl full of water.

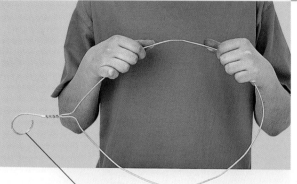

You may need an adult's help to bend the hook

2 Bend the wire coat hanger into a round shape. Bend in the hook so that it is closed up.

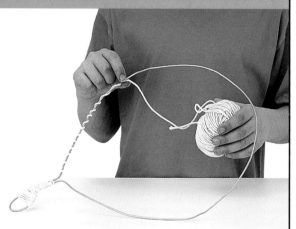

3 Wind string tightly around the hook, and then coil it around the rest of the coat hanger.

4 Secure the string by wrapping electrical tape around the hook. You now have a bubble wand.

5 Dip the bubble wand into the bowl. Make sure that all of the string is covered with the mixture.

6 Remove the bubble wand and let some of the mixture drip off.

Can you keep the bubble wand moving to make a long sausage shape?

Twist the bubble wand sharply to make a free-floating bubble

7 Make bubbles by moving the bubble wand through the air. How big can you make them?

Stretchy water

Water molecules hold themselves together by surface tension. Washing-up liquid weakens the surface tension, allowing water to be stretched into thin film. A free-floating bubble filled with air will always form a sphere. This is because the surface tension is pulling it back into shape, just like a rubber balloon.

Magnet **test**
Experiment with magnetism

You will need:

- 2 bar magnets
- horseshoe magnet
- objects to test, for example: plastic spoon, coins, foil, pencil, paper clip

Magnet magic

All magnets have two ends with opposite forces to one another. These are called the north and south poles. The opposite poles of two magnets will attract each other. The same poles will repel (push each other way). Magnets attract things that are made of, or contain, iron or steel.

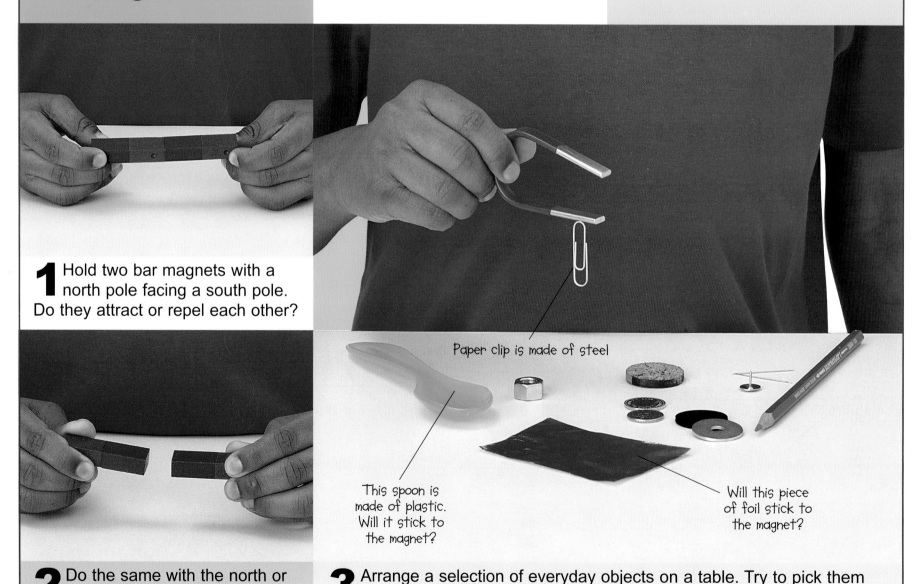

1 Hold two bar magnets with a north pole facing a south pole. Do they attract or repel each other?

Paper clip is made of steel

This spoon is made of plastic. Will it stick to the magnet?

Will this piece of foil stick to the magnet?

2 Do the same with the north or south poles facing each other. What happens?

3 Arrange a selection of everyday objects on a table. Try to pick them up with your magnet. Which ones are attracted to the magnet? Which ones does it not pick up?

Kissing fish

Make magnetic fish

You will need:

- card
- 2 sewing needles
- magnet
- water
- bowl or plate
- tape • scissors
- pen or pencil

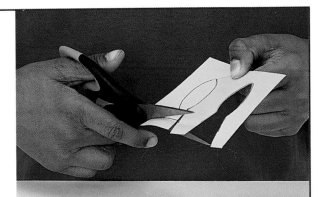

1 Cut out two fish shapes from the card. You could decorate them if you wish.

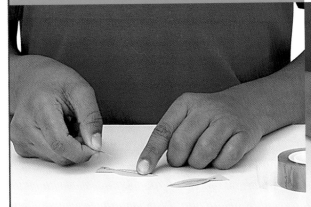

2 Tape the needles along the lengths of the fish.

3 Rub the needles with the magnet 20 times. Rub towards the nose of one fish and the tail of the other.

4 Fill your plate or bowl with water, and float the fish on top. What happens?

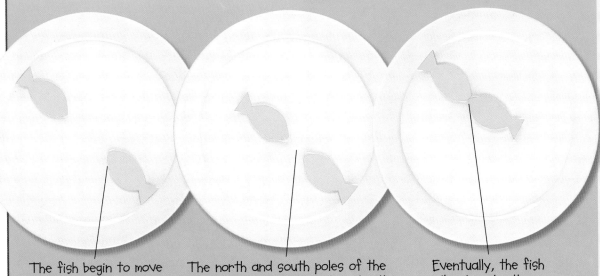

The fish begin to move towards each other

The north and south poles of the magnetized needles attract each other

Eventually, the fish 'kiss' each other

Making magnets

Stroking the needles with a magnet turns them into magnets. They have north and south poles, just like the bar magnets, and these attract and repel each other in exactly the same way. The magnetic attraction is strong enough to pull the fish toward each other across the water.

Floating compass

Find north with a needle

You will need:

- magnet
- sewing needle
- piece of thin card
- tape
- plate or bowl
- water
- compass
- scissors

1 Cut out a circle of card about five cm across. Tape the needle along the middle.

2 Stroke the needle with the magnet about 20 times in the same direction.

3 Fill the plate or bowl with water and float the card and needle on top. What happens?

The ends of the needle will point in a north–south direction

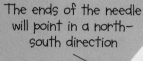

Use the compass to check the direction of your floating needle

Pole pointer

The magnetised needle, like all magnets, has a north and south pole. These line up with the Earth's north and south poles.

Lemon battery

Make electricity with fruit

You will need:

- lemon
- 2 pieces of wire with exposed ends
- copper coin
- nickel coin

Fruit power

The acid in the lemon and the different metals in the coins create a chemical reaction that makes electricity. Batteries contain plates of different metals surrounded by acid to make electrical current.

You can feel a tiny amount of electricity on your tongue

The coins react with the acid in the lemon and make an electrical current

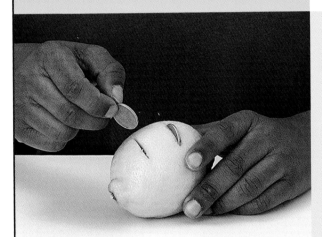

1 Ask an adult to cut two slits in the lemon. Push the coins into the slits as shown.

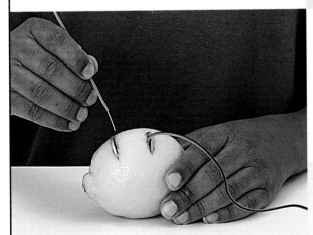

2 Push a coin into each slit and an exposed end of wire next to each coin.

3 Hold the two free ends of the wires to your tongue. Can you feel a slight tingling sensation?

Radio waves

Transmit a radio signal

You will need:

- battery
- 2 pieces of wire with exposed ends
- electrical tape
- portable AM/FM radio

1 Attach a piece of wire to one of the battery contacts with a piece of electrical tape.

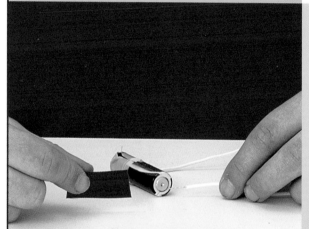

2 Attach the second piece of wire to the other contact.

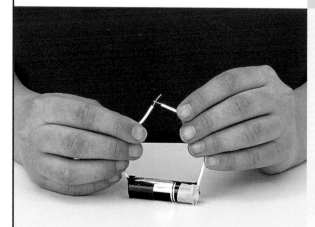

3 Touch the two free ends of the wires together. You should see a tiny spark.

Spark signals

Radio signals are produced by electrical currents, which travel through the air in waves. You have made a tiny radio transmitter that sends its own radio signal when you make the spark.

The radio picks up the signal as a crackling noise. This is created by the battery's electrical current.

Touching the wires together creates a spark.

4 Switch on the radio and select the AM band. Tune it so that it is not receiving any station. Hold the battery a short distance away from the radio and touch the wires together. What can you hear?

Static sparker

Make your own lightning

You will need:

- metal tray
- modelling clay
- polythene
(such as a dustbin liner)
- metal object
(a key, for example)

1 Lay the polythene on a table and put the tray on top. Press some modelling clay onto the tray.

2 Make the room dark and rub the tray across the top of the polythene for about 30 seconds.

3 Lift the tray off the polythene, leaving one corner close to the table. Bring the key close the tray.

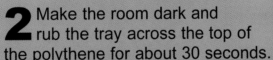
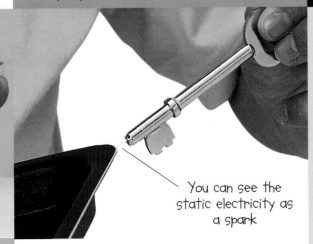
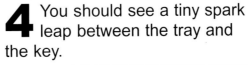

You can see the static electricity as a spark

4 You should see a tiny spark leap between the tray and the key.

Lightning leap

Rubbing the tray on the polythene creates static electricity. The tray has a negative charge and the key has a positive charge. This difference makes the electricity jump from the tray to the key. Lightning hits the ground because the bottom of a thunder cloud is negatively charged and the ground is positive.

59

Balloon **power**

Explore static electricity

You will need:

- balloons
- sweater or t-shirt
- a friend
- tissue paper

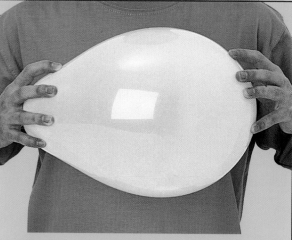

1 For all of these experiments, 'charge' the balloons by rubbing them against your t-shirt or sweater.

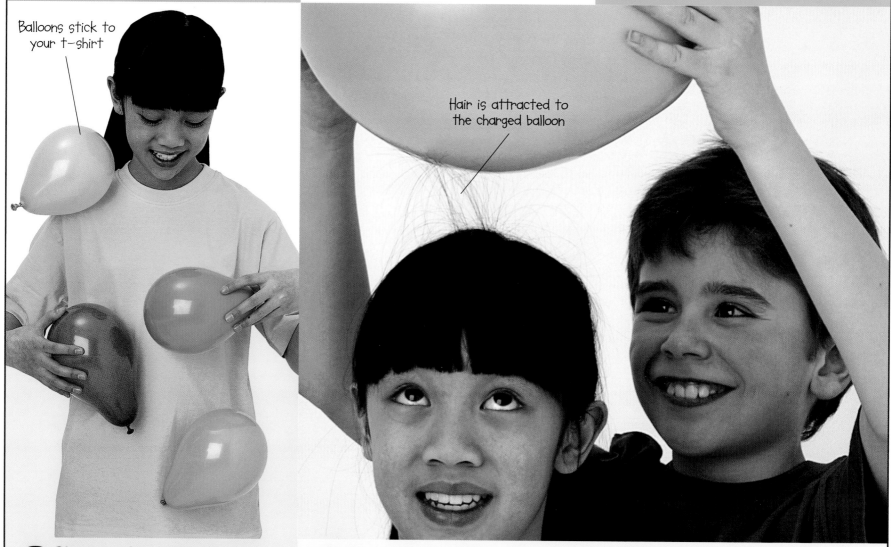

Balloons stick to your t-shirt

Hair is attracted to the charged balloon

2 Charge a few balloons. Can you make them stick to yourself or a friend?

3 Try holding a charged balloon over a friend's hair. Can you make it stick to the balloon? This works best if your friend has long, fine hair.

Positive and negative

Rubbing the balloon gives it a negative electrical charge. It is attracted to the positive charge on you, your friend's hair, and the paper.

4 Tear up some tissue paper into lots of small pieces.

Tissue paper jumps onto the charged balloon

5 Lay the tissue paper pieces on a table. Charge a balloon and hold it over the pieces of paper. Can you make them jump to the balloon?

Balloon **power**

Move things with a balloon

You will need:

- balloons
- sweater or t-shirt
- empty drinks can
- tap

Moving particles

Everything is made of atoms, which contain tiny particles called protons and electrons. Protons are always positive and electrons are negative. Rubbing the balloon moves electrons onto it, and it becomes negatively charged. The parts of the water and drinks can closest to the balloon get a positive charge, and are attracted to it.

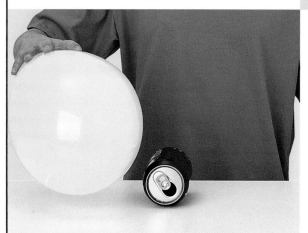

1 Put the can on a table on its side. Hold a charged balloon about 30 cm away from it.

2 Can you make the can roll towards the balloon?

The uncharged balloon has no effect on the water

3 Turn on a tap to get a very fine stream of water. Hold an uncharged balloon near it.

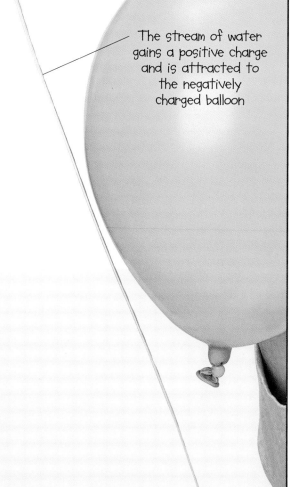

The stream of water gains a positive charge and is attracted to the negatively charged balloon

4 Now do the same with a charged balloon. What happens?

Static snake

Charm a paper snake

You will need:

- tissue paper
- pencil
- scissors
- plastic pen
- piece of wool

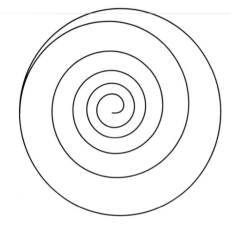

1 Copy this spiral shape onto a piece of tissue paper.

2 Carefully cut out the shape. Ask an adult to help you if necessary.

Snake charmer

Rubbing the pen makes it negatively charged, just like the balloons were in the 'Balloon power' experiments. As you touch the tissue paper snake, its positive charge makes it stick to the pen.

3 Rub the plastic pen about 20 times with the piece of wool.

4 Hold the tip of the pen close to middle of the spiral snake. Can you make the snake rise towards it?

A-maze-ing plant

See a plant grow towards light

You will need:

- flower pot full of soil
- runner bean seed
- saucer • shoe box
- 2 pieces of card
(the same width and depth as the shoe box)
- water
- scissors
- jug

1 Soak the bean seed in water overnight. Plant it in the soil, about halfway down the pot.

2 Water the seed well. If your pot has holes in the bottom, keep it on a saucer.

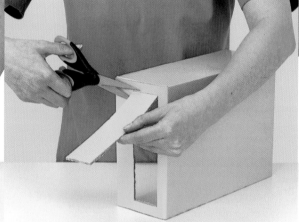

3 Cut a large, rectangular window in one end of the shoe box.

4 Cut out a small window toward the end of each piece of card.

5 Put the pot and one card window in the box. It should be on the opposite side to the pot.

6 Close the box and keep it in a sunny place. Check the bean and water it regularly.

The second window should be opposite to the first

7 When the plant has grown through the first card window, put in the second one.

64

8 Close the box, put it back in the sunny place, and leave it for another few days.

Sun seekers

All plants need sunlight to make food. That is why the runner bean plant grows towards the light through the card maze. In a forest, trees will compete with each other to reach the light. The redwood trees shown in the picture above can grow as high as 90 metres.

The plant grows towards the sunlight

The plant follows the direction of the sunlight coming through the windows

Colour flowers

Make a white flower coloured

You will need:

- white flowers (carnations are best)
- tall glasses
- scissors
- water
- food colouring (at least two colours)

2 Cut the stems of the flowers about 10 cm from the end.

4 Take another flower and split the stem up towards the flower head.

1 Fill three glasses about two-thirds full of water. Add some food colouring to each glass.

3 Put one flower in each of the glasses and leave them somewhere to stand overnight.

5 Put one half of the split stem in one coloured water and the other half in a different colour.

Red

Yellow

Red and white

Red and blue

Standing a flower in two colours makes a two-coloured flower head

Deep drinkers

Plants, like all living things, need to drink water to survive. This experiment shows how flowers get their water from the ground. The coloured water is sucked up through the stems and into the petals.

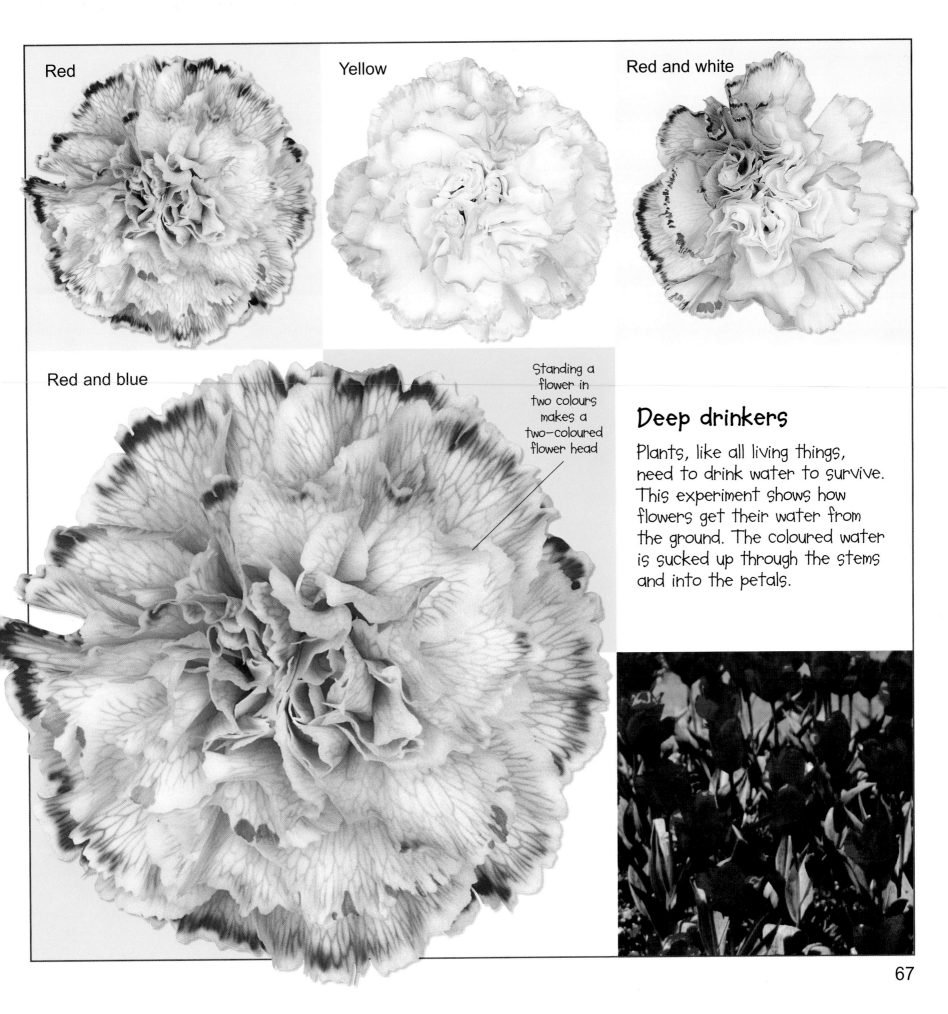

Paper petals

Give a paper flower a drink

You will need:

- white paper
- colouring pens
- scissors
- plate
- water

1 Draw this flower shape onto a piece of paper, but make it about twice the size it is here.

2 Colour in the flower. Use whichever colours you like best.

3 Carefully cut around the petals of the flower.

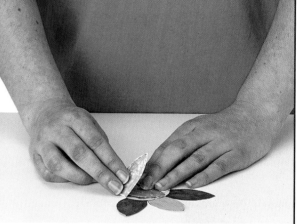

4 Carefully fold in the petals, one on top of the other.

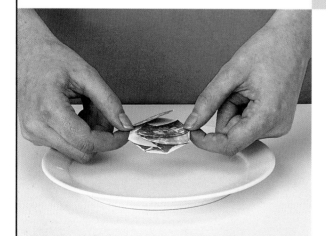

5 Pour some water onto the plate, and float the flower in the middle. What happens?

Thirsty flowers

In dry weather, when flowers are short of water, they usually close up their petals. After a shower of rain, the petals will open up, just like those on your paper flower.

Tulip with closed petals

The tulip opens up when watered

The paper soaks up the water

The paper expands and the flower opens up

Eventually, the flower opens up completely

Sunset bowl

See your own sunset

You will need:

- glass bowl full of water
  - torch
  - milk
- teaspoon
- dark room

Sky colours

Light from the Sun is made up of lots of colours. At sunset, when the Sun is low in the sky, the light passes at an angle through tiny bits of water and dust in the air, which block out the blue and green parts of the light. This is why we see a red sky. With the Sun high in the sky during the day, the sky looks blue.

The milky water stops some of the light getting through. We only see the red and orange parts

1 Add two to three teaspoons of milk to the water and give it a stir. Turn on your torch and shine it into the bowl from one side. What do you see?

Indoor rainbow

Make a rainbow without rain

You will need:

- water
- mirror
- dish
- torch
- white card
- modelling clay

Rainbow colours

We see a rainbow when it is sunny and raining at the same time. The raindrops reflect the sunlight and split it into the colours that make white light. They are: red, orange, yellow, green, blue, indigo and violet. This experiment creates the same effect, as the light reflected from the mirror passes through the water.

The water splits the reflected light into several colours

1 Fill half of the dish with water. Rest the mirror against one end of the dish and secure it with modelling clay. Shine the torch at the mirror through the water, while holding the card above. What do you see?

Sun dial

Tell the time with the Sun

You will need:

- white card
- sharp pencil
- scissors
- pen
- area of soft ground outside
- a sunny day!

1 Cut out a circle from the card, about 15 cm in diameter.

2 Make a hole in the centre of the card with a sharp pencil. Ask an adult to help you if necessary.

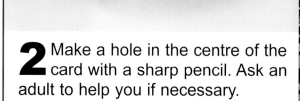

3 Push the pencil into an area of soft ground. Put it in a place that gets plenty of sunlight.

Mark the times and positions of the shadows with a pen

The shadow moves as the Sun's position in the sky changes

11 o'clock

10 o'clock

9 o'clock

The pencil casts a shadow across the card

Moving shadows

The shadow on the sun dial moves according to the position of the Sun in the sky. This changes as the Earth spins around. When the Sun is at its highest point in the sky – about noon – the shadow will be quite short. In the morning and late afternoon, when the Sun is lower, the shadow will be longer.

Rising heat

How does heat move?

You will need:

- 2 plastic drinks bottles
- food colouring
- 4 cm x 4 cm piece of card
- hot and cold water
- bowl

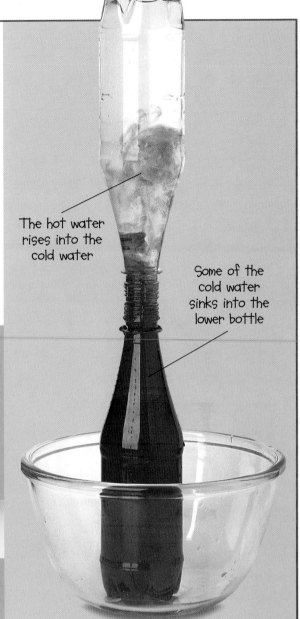

The hot water rises into the cold water

Some of the cold water sinks into the lower bottle

Do this experiment in a bowl

1 Fill one bottle with cold water, and one with hot. Add some food colouring to the hot water.

2 Place the piece of card on top of the bottle of cold water, and hold it firmly in position.

3 Carefully turn the bottle of cold water upside down, and put it on top of the other bottle.

4 Make sure that the bottles are lined up. Ask an adult to help you take out the piece of card.

Convection currents

Heat always moves from a hot place to a cold place. The hot water molecules are moving around more than the cold water molecules, which means that the hot water expands and moves into the cold water. This movement is called convection. This is how heat moves in all liquids and gases.

Bottle tornado

Make a whirling water vortex

You will need:

- 2 plastic drinks bottles
- rubber washer (same size as the bottle opening)
- electrical tape
- water
- food colouring (optional)

1 Fill one of the bottles about two-thirds full of water. Add some food colouring if you wish.

2 Put the washer over the mouth of the filled bottle. Tape it in place, leaving the hole open.

Forces and pressure

The water is held in the top bottle by the air pressure in the lower bottle, and the surface tension of the water in the washer. Spinning the bottle creates a turning force in the water that breaks the surface tension, allowing the water to flow. The air in the lower bottle is then forced into the top.

3 Balance the mouth of the second bottle on top of the washer. Fasten the two bottles together with electrical tape.

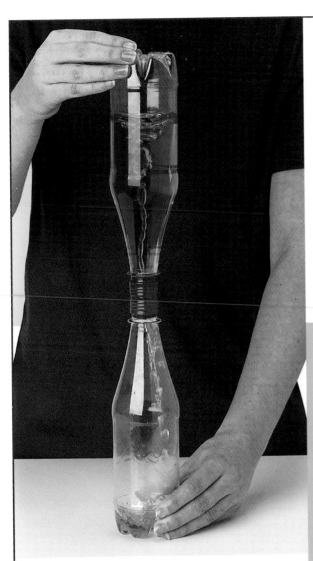

Water or air moving like this is called a vortex

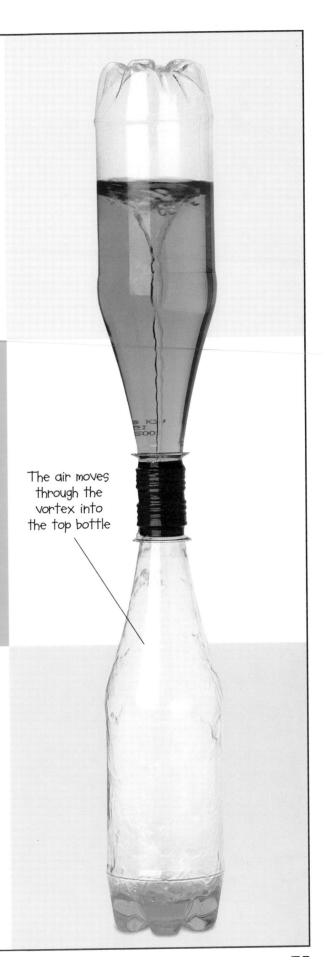

The air moves through the vortex into the top bottle

4 Turn the bottles over. Hold the base of the empty bottle, and move the top one in rapid circles.

5 Let go of the bottles, and the water should flow into the bottom.

Turning tornadoes

Tornadoes are made by funnels of warm air rising from the ground being made to spin by strong winds. The pressure inside the tornado is much lower than the air around it, which is why they suck things up like a huge vacuum cleaner. Tornadoes can twist at speeds of up to 800 km/h.

Glossary

Words in **bold** are explained in this glossary

Acid
A type of **chemical** that can eat away at substances. Weak acids are found in everyday things such as lemon juice and have a bitter taste. An **indicator** turns red when mixed with an acid.

Aerodynamic
Something that flies well through the air has an aerodynamic shape. This is because its design reduces the effect of **drag**.

Aerofoil
The curved shape of an aeroplane wing. Its shape creates the **force** of **lift**, which gets the aeroplane off the ground.

Air pressure
The **force** with which air presses down and pushes against things.

Alkali
The **chemical** opposite of an **acid**. Alkalis **dissolve** in water, and cancel out, or neutralize, the effect of an **acid**. An **indicator** turns blue when mixed with an alkali.

Atom
The smallest part of an **element**. Everything around us, in the world and throughout the universe, is made up of atoms.

Attract
The invisible **force** that pulls **magnets** toward each other. The north **pole** of one **magnet** attracts the south **pole** of another **magnet**.

Balance
A position where something has equal weight on either side. The point where something balances is called the centre of **gravity**.

Balanced forces
When two opposing **forces** push or pull against or away from each other to keep something in one position. A bridge stays up and supports things because of balanced forces pushing and pulling throughout its structure.

Battery
A source of **electricity**. **Electric current** is created in batteries by two different materials (usually zinc and another metal) reacting with an **acid**.

Carbon dioxide
A **gas** that is breathed out by people and animals. It is also made by some chemical reactions, such as when bicarbonate of soda and vinegar mix together.

Chemical
A single, pure substance. A chemical can be changed when it is mixed with another substance.

Chromatography
A way of separating a mixture into its different ingredients by passing it through something. For example, separating out the colours in sweets by running them through blotting paper.

Condensation
When a **gas** turns into a **liquid**, usually by cooling down.

Conduction
The movement of heat through a **solid**.

Convection
The movement of heat through a **liquid** or a **gas**.

Density
How tightly packed together the material inside something is, relative to its size. For example, the material inside a small, heavy marble is very tightly packed together – it has a high density. A large, empty box has a low density.

Dissolve
When something breaks up into very small parts in a **liquid**. For example, sugar dissolves easily in water.

Drag
The **force** that slows down an object as it moves through a **liquid** or **gas**. For example, a parachute is slowed down by the drag of the air pushing against it.

Electrical charge
What is produced when an **atom** loses or gains **electrons**. Rubbing a balloon **attracts electrons** to it, giving it a negative charge. When something loses **electrons**, it gains a positive charge.

Electric current
The rate at which **electrical charge** moves.

Electricity
A type of **energy** created by **electrons** moving from one place to another. **Static electricity** occurs naturally, but the electricity we use at home is generated in power stations.

Electron
A **particle** of an **atom** with a negative **electrical charge**.

Element
A substance made up of one kind of **atom**. An **element** cannot be broken up into something else.

Emulsion
When the droplets of one **liquid** are suspended in another without **dissolving** into it. For example, adding some washing-up liquid to a glass filled with oil and water makes an emulsion.

Energy
This can be described as the 'ability to do work.' Energy comes in many forms, including light, heat, and electrical energy.

Evaporation
When a **liquid** changes into a **gas**, usually when it heats up.

Force
A push or pull. A force can 'do work,' such as speeding things up, slowing them down, or changing their shape.

Gas
A substance that will expand to fill any space that it occupies.

Gravity
The **force** that makes things pull toward each other. Big, heavy things have lots of gravity. The Earth's gravity pulls everything toward its surface.

Indicator
A substance used to test the strength of an **acid** or an **alkali**. Red cabbage juice is an indicator. It changes colour according to the strength of the **acid** or **alkali** that is being tested .

Lift
The **force** created by the **aerofoil** of an aeroplane wing. It lifts the plane up into the air.

Liquid
A substance with loosely arranged **particles**, which allow it to move and spread out.

Magnet
A metal object that can pull iron, or anything containing iron (steel, for example) towards it. It can also **attract** and **repel** other magnets.

Magnetic field
The area around a **magnet** inside which iron will be pulled toward it.

Molecule
Two or more **atoms** joined together to create a new **particle** of a substance that can exist on its own.

Particle
Used generally to describe tiny parts of things. **Molecules, atoms** and **electrons** are all called particles.

Pigment
A substance that is added to something to give it colour. We see the colours in paints and inks because of the pigments that have been added to them.

Pole
One of the two opposite ends of a **magnet**. They are called north and south poles.

Proton
A particle of an **atom** with a positive **electrical charge**.

Reflection
The way that light bounces off something, such as a mirror.

Refraction
The way that light is bent as it passes from one substance to a different one, such as from air to water.

Repel
The invisible **force** that pushes the north **pole** of one **magnet** away from the north **pole** of another. South poles also repel each other.

Solid
A substance that keeps its shape.

Static electricity
A type of **electricity** produced when two things rub together.

Surface tension
A **force** that pulls together the **molecules** on the surface of a **liquid**.

Vibration
When something moves backwards and forwards very quickly.

Vortex
A whirling movement in air or water that pulls everything to its middle. For example, a tornado.

Weight
The **force** on an object caused by **gravity** pulling on it.

Index